SNOWPLOWS

SNOWPLOWS

Illustrated with photographs

Hope Irvin Marston

Dodd, Mead & Company

New York

The photographs in this book are used by permission and through the courtesy of: Amtrak (Ira Silverman), 36; Balderson, Inc., 26, 28, 32; *Constructioneer*, 43; Craig, 27; Deere & Co., 17, 18, 19, 20, 21, 22 (right); Fair Manufacturing, Inc., 45; Frink America, 25, 29; Gravely International, Inc., 22 (left); Livingston Lansing, 10; Hope Irvin Marston, 16; Oshkosh Truck Corporation, 31, 35; Rolba Company Limited, 33; Rugg Manufacturing Company, 14; *Seaway Review*, 41; Snowblast, 30, 34; Transport Canada Photo, 40; Union Pacific Railroad Museum Collection, 37, 38, 39; Walter Truck Corp., 46; *Watertown* (New York) *Daily Times*, 6, 8, 9, 11, 13, 15, 23, 44; Weldo (Alberta) Limited, 24; Weston Bodies, Inc., 42.

1   2   3   4   5   6   7   8   9   10

Library of Congress Cataloging-in-Publication Data

Marston, Hope Irvin.
Snowplows.

Includes index.
Summary: Text and photographs describe various types
of snow removal equipment and how they work.
1. Snow removal—Equipment and supplies—Juvenile
literature.   2. Snow plows—Juvenile literature.
[1. Snow plows.   2. Snow removal] I. Title.
TD868.M37   1986   628'.466   86-8935
ISBN 0-396-08818-X

For Roberta and Rich

Winter is a fun time for boys and girls in the northern states. Bundled up in jackets, boots, colorful scarves, and warm mittens, they head outdoors. They slide and ski and skate. They make jolly snowmen, or lovely snow "angels." They pelt each other with snowballs. They chase one another in lively games of Fox and Geese.

Their cheeks and noses turn red. Their fingers and toes tingle with the cold. Then they race back to their warm houses to "thaw" themselves out.

Meanwhile, the snow and ice outside can cause big trouble.

Snow and ice on highways cause traffic accidents.

In towns and cities, travelers are stranded.

Too much snow stops deliveries, and closes businesses. It sometimes causes roofs to collapse. It halts fire trucks and ambulances.

It buries automobiles, and people are "snowed in" and cannot leave their homes.

What can be done to keep things moving? Before the snow gets that deep, it is time to bring out the snowplows.

Snow falls in every state. In recent years, states that usually receive only a trace of snow have been getting much more. That causes problems. There is no equipment to move the snow. Drivers panic because they don't know how to drive in it. There are many accidents.

Most northern states receive several hundreds of inches of snow each year. Their local and state highway crews have special equipment to remove both snow and ice promptly. The people are used to dealing with snow.

Whether it is clearing a sidewalk or a railroad track or an airport runway, there is equipment to do the job.

The quickest way to get rid of snow on a sidewalk or driveway is to shovel it. Snow shovels are made of steel or aluminum. They have handles about three feet long. Children's shovels are smaller. Often they are made of plastic.

A "backsaver" is a snow shovel with a gooseneck bend in the handle. The bend makes it easier to shovel without tiring. The "backsaver" can be used to push snow if you don't want to lift it.

Backsaver

Snow Scoop

Children's Snow Shovel

Sidewalk Scrapers

Snow Pusher

Hard-packed snow or ice can be chipped loose with a sidewalk scraper. Light snow can be pushed along with a snow pusher. Or with a snow scoop, a big 30″ x 24″ pusher that slides along on runners.

You don't have to lift so much snow when you use a snow scoop or a pusher. The less you have to lift, the better. Many people suffer heart attacks each winter while shoveling snow.

Some fellows will do anything to get out of shoveling snow. A blade attached to a bike will work.

Snow and ice are heavy. When they pile up on your roof, you must get them off. The snow melt can damage the ceilings below. The weight of the snow and ice can collapse the roof.

To get rid of the buildup of snow and ice, you need a ladder, a shovel, perhaps a hoe, a scraper, lots of muscle, and steady nerves.

Snow and ice must be removed from cars for safety's sake. We need to see clearly in stormy weather.

Snow is brushed off the car, and the headlights and taillights uncovered. Ice on the windows and windshield is cleaned off with an ice scraper.

Light snow can be blown away with a backpack power blower. This blower can also be used for clearing snow from steps, or in other places where a larger blower won't fit.

Shoveling snow is hard work. It takes a lot of time, too. In places where lots of heavy snow falls, snow throwers and snowblowers make the work easier. This girl is operating a snow thrower.

A snow thrower has paddles that pull in the snow as the machine is pushed forward. It can throw snow up to 18 feet. It's great for cleaning driveways or sidewalks.

A snowblower has spiral blades that turn like a giant screw to pick up the snow. A fan then blows the snow out— as far as 60 feet. Snowblowers can handle deeper, heavier snow than snow throwers.

Both throwers and blowers allow the operator to choose where the snow will go when it is blown out.

But clearing away snow with a snowblower is a cold job. A walk-under cab provides protection from the flying snow.

The more snow there is, the bigger job it is to get rid of it. Blades or blowers can be attached to tractors of various sizes.

This small garden tractor (left) has a four-foot blade attached. The farm tractor has a snowblower.

Because of the weight of blades or blowers, tire chains are often used to keep the wheels from spinning.

A tractor with a bucket loader can move heavy snow.
The bucket scoops up the snow and dumps it on a pile
where it is out of the way, or onto a truck if it must be
carried away.

Areas that get lots of snow each winter must have tough equipment to get rid of it. Large, heavy blades are mounted on trucks or road graders.

A one-way blade plow is used when snow must be cast (thrown) to one side only.

A reversible blade plow can be set to cast snow either to the right or to the left.

A V-plow casts the snow to the left and to the right at the same time. It is useful where there is plenty of room for snow along both sides of the road.

Snow "wings" are large blades, 12 to 14 feet long. They can be mounted on the left or right or both sides of a road grader or a truck. They are raised or lowered by hydraulics.

A blade plow is used on the front of the vehicle. The wing pushes the snow away and levels it. That keeps it from falling back onto the highway.

Graders are used to scrape dirt roads during the summer. They move slowly. Yet they work well in winter with blades and wings attached to them.

This is the rear view of a grader with a V-plow in front and a right wing assembly attached.

Front view of a V-plow and one wing.

Rear view of a similar combination.

A rotary snowblower is useful for cutting through deep snowbanks. Large rotary blowers are used to clear country roads blocked with avalanche snow. They can remove as much as 1,750 tons of snow per hour.

The Oshkosh company builds some of the toughest self-propelled rotary snowblowers. This giant "snow-eater" is almost 13 feet tall and 8½ feet wide. Its huge blades can "chew" through 50 tons of snow per minute.

In snowbelt areas, airport runways get buried with snow. Railroad tracks get covered over. As the temperature drops lower and lower, waterways freeze. Powerful equipment is needed to remove snow and ice.

Clearing an airport runway is a big task. A giant blade plow like this one (opposite) will move a lot of snow in a hurry. The huge rotary snowblower (above) gobbles up the snow and blows it out of the way.

Both rotary and blade plows are used to clear heavy snow from runways. Then a runway sweeper, called an "airport broom," moves in. The huge broom "sweeps" a path 12 to 15 feet wide. It picks up snow, water, debris, and dirt.

This mammoth model is 30 feet long, weighs 16 tons, and has 495 horsepower.

What about ice on the runway? Tank trucks to the rescue. They are the first weapon against ice.

Tankers hold 4,000 gallons of a special melting solution. Sprayer bars mounted at the rear of the tanker spread the solution a width of 40 feet. The melting solution can prevent the buildup of ice and snow if applied before a storm.

Railroad tracks buried with snow must be cleared to keep trains on schedule. Icy tracks are hazardous.

Many locomotives are equipped with a V-shaped plow on the front. The plow pushes the snow off to the sides of the tracks. The speed of the train blows the snow away as it passes. The heavy weight of the train breaks up any ice that may have formed.

Some railroad companies use heating elements called switch heaters to melt snow and ice at switching points. But even with plows and switch heaters, local track crews are needed to keep snow and ice from the rails.

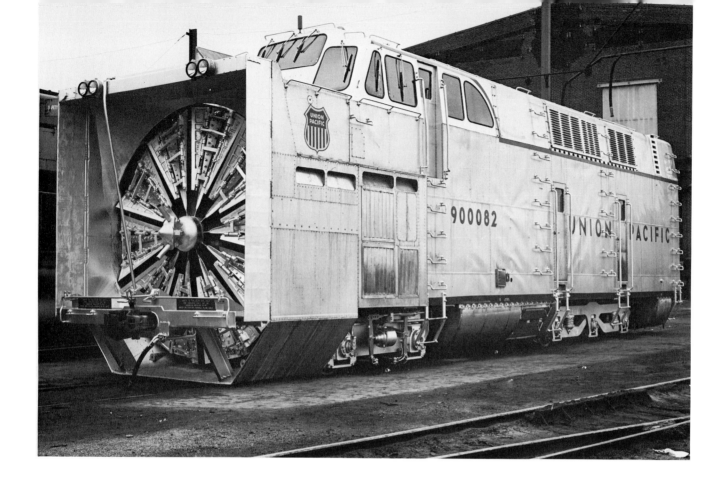

In areas such as our Rocky Mountains, giant rotary snowplows are powerful weapons against snow on the tracks. This locomotive has a rotary blade that is 12 feet in diameter. It can burrow through hard-packed, wind-driven snow that is 26 feet deep.

The Union Pacific Railroad has an unusual plow called a "snow melter." The snow melter is coupled to a train engine. It can plow through drifts six to eight feet high. The snow is carried up into a tank where it melts into water. Later the water is drained out.

Snow and ice choke rivers and block shipping lanes in canals and in the Great Lakes. Shippers cannot move their cargo.

Special ships, called icebreakers, are used to free vessels trapped in the ice. Icebreakers are built short in length and wide in the beam. They can ride up on the ice and crush it. They must not use too much fuel. Often they have to work for long periods in areas far from fuel supplies.

Ice on the highways is another winter hazard. Some places that get little snow have a big problem with ice.

Local supplies determine what is used to melt the ice. Salt and sand are used for slick, slippery roads. Coal states may use cinders or ashes. Chemicals are also used.

Sand and salt are spread on icy roads by trucks called sanders or spreaders. Or by a hopper like this one, with a funnel-shaped opening at the rear.

There are several kinds of sanders. All work the same way. Whatever is to be spread is carried in the body of the truck. It passes through a screen, and drops onto the highway at the rear of the vehicle. The driver controls how fast it comes out.

Sanders may have plows or wings attached to them. They can then plow and sand at the same time.

Dump trucks are important in snow removal. Especially in cities, snow must be trucked away. It has to be loaded and carried to open spaces or to a river where it can be dumped.

A modern snowblower like this one can fill a 10-wheel dump truck in a minute.

Wet snow is heavy, but it is lighter than most cargo usually carried by dump trucks. A large box, called a "body insert," can be fitted to a truck body. With it, the truck can carry three times the amount of snow in one trip that it could carry without it. This means fewer trips, and a saving in time, fuel, and money.

Have you ever heard of a snow-fighting school? There's one in New York State. Students attend lectures, practice on different types of snowplows, and even compete in a snowplowing contest.

The next time you meet a snowplow or a sand truck, give the driver a friendly smile and a wave. His work is difficult, and sometimes dangerous. But he is doing it for you.

Glossary

AIRPORT BROOM—A runway sweeper

BACKPACK POWER BLOWER—A compact blower used to clear light snow from cars and tight places where a shovel or a large blower won't fit

BACKSAVER—A shovel with a gooseneck handle

BLADE PLOW—A snowplow with a blade for pushing snow

BODY INSERT—A box put inside a truck body to increase cargo space

BUCKET LOADER—A scoop mounted on the front of a tractor or other equipment

GRADER—A machine for leveling roadways

HOPPER—A truck with a large box with a funnel-shaped opening

ICEBREAKER—A heavy ship built for crushing ice in frozen waterways

REVERSIBLE BLADE PLOW—A snowplow with a blade that can be set to cast snow to the left or right

ROTARY SNOWBLOWER—A blower with a blade that turns like a giant screw

RUNWAY SWEEPER—A giant brush for sweeping airport runways

SANDER—A truck with a screen that sifts sand and deposits it on icy highways

SCRAPER—A hand tool for scraping ice

SNOW MELTER—A machine used to clear snow from railroad tracks

SNOW PUSHER—A long-handled shovel for pushing snow

SNOW SCOOP—A two-handled pusher that slides on runners

SNOW THROWER—A machine with paddles used to clear light snow

SNOWBELT—Any area that normally receives a lot of snow

SNOWBLOWER—A machine with a spiral blade and a fan that picks up snow and blows it away

SPREADER—A truck that spreads sand or salt on icy roads

SWITCH HEATER—A device used for melting snow and ice at switch points on railroads

TANKERS—Tank trucks used to spray chemicals on airport runways

V-PLOW—A plow shaped like a V that throws snow in two directions at the same time

WINGS—Large blades which push back snow as it is plowed

Index